OTHER YEARLING BOOKS YOU WILL ENJOY:

Eleanor Clymer

SANTIAGO'S SILVER MINE

Illustrated by Ingrid Fetz

A Yearling Book

Published by
Dell Publishing
a division of
Bantam Doubleday Dell Publishing Group, Inc.
666 Fifth Avenue
New York, New York 10103

ISBN: 0-440-40157-7

Printed in the United States of America

April 1989

10 9 8 7 6 5 4 3

CW

For Jane Emily

SANTIAGO'S SILVER MINE

1

My name is Santiago. I live in a village in Mexico called San Juan de la Montaña.

I have a friend Andreas. We go everywhere together, and we do lots of things. Andreas is younger than I am, but he has many ideas that no one else has. And the thing I am going to tell about happened because of one of his ideas. It was that we should try to become rich.

Maybe it was foolish for two boys to want to be rich. But we had a good reason. You see, the harvest was very bad. My father could not earn enough for our family. And neither could Andreas' father. They are both farmers.

Our village is in the mountains. That's why it is called San Juan de la Montaña. Wherever you look there are mountains and more mountains. Our village is in a valley between two of them. It is quite small, just a few streets. There is a school and a place where the women wash clothes and a fountain where we all go for water. And we have a beautiful church. It is built of pink stone, with angels and flowers carved on the outside. Inside there are beautiful paintings and gold angels and a very big altar covered with gold paint. And the saints and the Virgin are dressed in silk and velvet.

You might think, seeing such a church, that our village is very rich. But it is not so. We could not be rich with such fields as we have. They are on the hillsides, and the soil washes down with the rain.

No, the reason we have this church is that once there was a mine here, a silver mine, up in the hills behind the village. The men of the village used to work there. My grandfather was one of them. The people who owned the mine were very rich, though not the ones who worked in it. It was the owners who had this church built.

The mine is closed now. They say there was no more silver, or at least not enough to bother about, or maybe they could not reach it. Anyhow, the owners went away. They left one man to guard the mine. His name was José. And they left us the church. We are glad to have it, because it is so beautiful.

Sometimes strangers would come here; not often, because the road was not good and they didn't like to drive their cars over mud or rocks. But sometimes they came to see the church, and if Andreas and I were around, we would ask them if they wanted to see the mine too. If they did, we took them by a path that led over a hill to a place where there was a stone wall. There was a big door in the wall, and we banged on it. José opened the door and let us in. He was always grouchy and never talked much. He was pretty old when we knew him, and had lived there all alone for a long time.

He had a little farm in there, a small hut, and a garden; a goat, a burro, and a dog. He showed all this to the tourists, and also the mine shaft and the entrance to the mine where the miners used to go in to dig out the ore. It was just a small mine. The ore used to be taken away to another place where they had machinery for getting the silver out.

Well, sometimes the tourists took pictures and gave José some money, and we went back to the village. Maybe they gave us money too and bought us some Coca-Cola from a little store that *Señora* Lopez, one of our neighbors, had in the front of her house. Then they drove away.

Otherwise it was very quiet here. I went to school and I helped my father. He raised corn on some land that belonged to everybody, because he did not have his own land. I would go with him to help him dig the field and plant the seed. Then later I helped with pulling weeds and with harvesting the corn.

I liked to work with my father. Of course it meant that sometimes I had to stay out of school.

And in fact I used to think it would be better for me to quit school altogether, so that I could earn money for the family.

But my father got angry at that. He shouted at me, "All my life I have worked hard and I did not go to school. Now you have a chance to go, so don't let me hear about quitting!"

Well, this year the harvest was poor. We planted the corn and then we waited for rain, but the rain did not come when it was supposed to. We went to the church and prayed, but it did no good. The corn came up very slowly. Then it did rain, but it rained too much. The corn was nearly washed away. Papa and I dug ditches for the water to run off. We hoed the earth to protect the corn. But when Papa looked at it, he said, "Santiago, there will only be enough corn for a couple of months."

I knew that was bad. The corn was the most important thing for us. In our house we eat corn for every meal. My mother grinds it for tortillas and soup and tamales—we would not know what to do without it.

One day Papa and I went up to the corn field to harvest the corn. We filled some bags and went down again. My mother was standing in the doorway waiting for us. My sister Maria was sewing under the plum tree. My little sister Rosita was playing in the dirt with a straw doll and some

pieces of wood. The chickens were walking around, and the goat was tied in the corral. It looked the same as it always did. But my parents were worried.

Mama said, "Well, how is it?"

Papa shook his head and said, "It won't be enough."

Mama asked, "What will you do?"

He answered, "I will go to the hacienda tomorrow."

The hacienda is a big estate near us. They have very large fields, and they need many workers.

So we ate our supper of tortillas and beans. Afterward I went out and met Andreas.

I said, "My father is going to the hacienda tomorrow."

He said, "Mine too."

So I understood that they had a poor harvest too. Many people did.

In the morning Papa and Andreas' father went to the hacienda. They got some work to do, but it only lasted a few days. The harvest was poor there too, and there was not enough work for many people.

Mama asked, "What will you do now?"

And Papa answered, "I will go to the town and see if I can get work."

So the next morning Mama got up very early and made tortillas, and Papa took his bag and went to the town. There he got a job on the roads, digging.

Mama worked too. She sold things; cactus fruit from our trees or eggs, sometimes a chicken. Or she washed for people.

I went to school, but my sister Maria stayed home to help with the work and to take care of Rosita.

I liked school, because we had a new teacher. He didn't just make us recite numbers and letters. He told us good stories. Sometimes he told about our ancestors, the Indians who lived in our country long ago before the Spaniards came. He told us about the great cities they built, and the carvings and paintings they made, the sculptures of stone

and clay and other wonderful things. He showed
us pictures of these things, and told us how they
were lost or forgotten for hundreds of years, and
then were discovered. It was so interesting, I felt
happy to be Mexican. I was having such a good
time, I hardly noticed anything, till one day I
came home from school, and there was Papa.

He was home early. He and Mama were talking
and they seemed very worried.

I said, "Papa, you are here!"

And he said, "Yes, there is no more work on the
roads."

Mama asked him, "What can we do now?"

And he answered, "The only thing to do is to go to Mexico City. There I can probably get a job."

I did not know what to think. It might be fun to go there and see all the sights. But Mama began to cry. She said, "No, no! We cannot go there!"

Papa got angry and said, "If I say we will go, we will go!" And he walked out of the house. But he really didn't want to go either. Mama told me why. She said that once before, they all went there, when Maria was little and I was a baby. And it was very bad. They went to live with my uncle. They thought he would have a fine place, but it was a shack, much worse than our house, and twelve people lived there.

Mama said, "Ay, I was afraid to go out. There were so many cars and so much noise, I thought I would be killed."

I asked her, "What did Papa do there?"

She said, "Your Papa got a job working in a factory where they made shoes. They didn't pay much and everything was so dear! We had to pay rent for a room, and all the food and firewood had to be bought. And Papa did not like the city, working for a boss. He likes the land. So finally we said, 'Well, it is bad at home in the village but at least we don't have to pay for a house or firewood, and maybe we can live there.' So we came home."

I understood then that Papa did not like to go to the city, but he had to. He decided to go by himself. In the morning, Mama gave him a bag with some tortillas and a clean shirt, and he started to walk. Andreas' father went with him. We stood in the road and watched them go, and I felt very sad.

I said, "I wish I could do something to help."

"Yes," said Andreas. "We will."

I was surprised. He didn't look sad at all. He seemed to have decided something.

I asked him, "What will we do?"

He said, "Oh, I don't know yet. But we'll do something. Things will get better soon."

I said, "Well, I hope so. They can't get worse."

2

But I was wrong. They did get worse.

First of all, it was lonesome after Papa went away. It was too quiet. I would rather have him shout at us once in a while than not be there.

And then, Mama went to the hacienda to do washing there, so when I came home from school there was only Maria and my little sister Rosita. I knew I should help Maria; she had all the work to do. She had to grind corn and fetch water and sweep and take care of Rosita. I did go for water, but it was so sad in the house, I didn't like it, so I looked for things to do outside.

Andreas and I tried to think of ways to earn

money. We went up on the hillsides and gathered firewood to sell to people. And we carried water from the fountain for people, because some women are too old to carry water. But they could only give us a few centavos.

I gave the money to Mama when she got home, but when she heard how I got it, she said, "You should carry water for old ladies for nothing."

We often didn't have enough to eat. Sometimes Mama would go to her aunt or her cousin to borrow some corn or beans. And sometimes, if she had some money, she would go to *Señora* Lopez to buy something from her store. One day she went there and came home with some squash and beans in her basket, but without her rebozo, her shawl. Maria asked her where it was, and she said, "Oh, I lent it to a woman whose baby was cold."

But we knew she had sold it. She put on her old one, which was full of holes.

That made me angry. It was getting colder, and we did not have enough clothes to wear anyhow.

Papa wrote that he had found a job in the city, working in a restaurant. Sometimes he carried boxes from the market, and sometimes he washed dishes. He sent us a little money in the letter. But it didn't last long.

I said to Andreas, "What can we do to earn money so our fathers can come home and our mothers will have food to give us?"

Andreas said, "Well, I have been thinking about it, and I know what to do."

I said, "You do? What is it?"

He answered, "We must find some treasure."

That made me laugh. "That's a good joke," I said. "Where can we find treasure?"

Andreas said, "Don't laugh. There must be treasure. The teacher said so."

I said, "You're crazy. I heard the teacher too, and he never said there was treasure. You are making it up."

But he insisted. "Don't you remember? He even showed us pictures. There were golden masks and necklaces and carved stones. He called them treasures. If we find some, we can sell them and we will be rich."

It seemed that he thought these things were everywhere; you just had to scratch the earth and you would find some.

The next day I asked the teacher about it. "Are there such things around our village?"

He said, "No, Santiago, there aren't. The things I told you about were found far away from here. Maybe when you are grown up you will go and see them."

I told Andreas he was mistaken. But he was not discouraged. He just said, "*Está bien*. Maybe we will find something else."

I said, "Maybe we will, but I don't think so."

Well, the next day we didn't go to school. We went with *Señor* Salvador, one of the neighbors, to his field to cut corn stalks. He did not pay us but he gave us some food for our dinner.

His field was on a hillside. When it was time to eat our dinner, we sat on some stones on the top of the hill. We could see the high mountains all

around, and the birds flying around in the blue sky. Looking down, we could see the village far below us. We could see the church and the houses, very small, like the toy houses children play with. And then, looking in another direction, we saw the entrance to the mine and José's little farm.

"I think I see José," said Andreas.

"You couldn't," I said. "It's too far away."

"Yes, I do," he insisted. "I can see him walking around. I wonder what he does in there."

"He works in his garden," said *Señor* Salvador. "He is an old man now; he doesn't need to do much."

Then Andreas got an idea. "I wonder if there is still silver in the mine?"

I said, "There couldn't be. If there were, the owners would not have left."

Andreas said, "Well, there may be a little. If not, why would they have left José there? I'd like to go down and see."

Señor Salvador laughed and said, "Poor old José, he has to stay there to keep foolish people from going in and getting killed. Come on now, it's time to go back to work."

So we said no more, but as we walked home later, Andreas said, "Tomorrow let's go and bang on the door and get a look inside the mine."

But when I got home, I forgot about it because something else had happened. Maria was sick. She coughed and had a pain in her chest.

Mama tried to cure her. She said Maria had a cold from going for water in the evening. She wrapped her in blankets and gave her medicine made from herbs. Maria got a little better, but not much.

So now I could not go to school. I had to stay home and take care of Rosita. She was four years old, too big for Mama to carry with her and too small to walk far or to play alone.

A week went by, and still Maria did not feel well. So Mama stayed home from her work. She thought Maria must be bewitched. She didn't know what to do, since Papa wasn't home. So she went to see *Tía* Clara.

Tía Clara is Mama's great-aunt, and she is Maria's godmother. She is very old and knows a lot. She came and looked at Maria and said, "She's growing too fast, that's all. She needs more food."

Well, that day Mama killed our last chicken, and we ate it. It was a good dinner. I knew I should not eat much, so that there would be more for Maria, but I was so hungry I could not help it.

The next day *Tía* Clara and Mama went to the church and lit a candle, and also made a silver offering. That is something we do here. It's called a *milagro*. You can buy a little silver arm or a leg or a heart, whichever part hurts, and you give it to the Virgin or one of the saints and pray for help.

Mama didn't have money for the *milagro,* so she borrowed it from *Tía* Clara. She bought a heart and pinned it to the skirt of the Virgin herself, and we all prayed. Andreas came along to help us pray. Afterward they went home, but Andreas and I stayed in the church.

I like to walk around and look at the church, because it is so beautiful. It makes me forget about being poor and having trouble. But the best thing about it is that the walls are covered with pictures. *Retablos,* we call them. They are paintings that people have put there to give thanks when somebody has been cured or saved from an accident.

Many of them were about things that happened in the mine, because there used to be accidents there very often. There were floods, or perhaps stones would fall from the roof, and a miner would get hurt. Some of the *retablos* were very

old. My favorite one is a picture of something that happened when my grandfather was working there.

I looked at the *retablos* and I thought about all those people who were saved, and I began to feel angry. I went and stood in front of my own saint, Santiago, the one I am named after, and I said, "Why can't you do something? My sister is sick and my father went away. Can't you help us?"

Then I began to feel frightened and thought I shouldn't be so rude, so I said, "All right. If my sister gets well, I will give a new *retablo* to the church."

I didn't know how I would get it, but somehow I would.

Then I went outside. The sun was bright after the darkness of the church. Andreas was waiting for me out on the steps, and when I came out, he pulled my arm and said, "Look!"

A car had arrived in the middle of the plaza. It was bright blue. Two people got out of it. I could see that they were strangers, foreigners, because their clothes looked new and they had cameras around their necks. The man called to us and asked, "Which is the road to the town? I think we are lost."

He spoke Spanish, but it sounded funny. However, we were polite and didn't laugh. I said that they had to go back and then go another way. They said, *"Gracias,"* but they did not start. They stood there looking up at the church.

I had an idea. I said, "Would you like to see the church?"

The woman said, *"Sí.* It is beautiful."

So we took them inside and showed them everything, the saints and the gold angels and the altar.

They looked at everything, saying, "How wonderful! How interesting!"

Then we showed them the *retablos,* and they examined the pictures, and the woman asked, "What does it all mean?"

So I tried to explain. I told them about the silver mine, and how the men in the village used to work there, deep down in tunnels under the ground, digging out the silver. And I told how there were accidents in the mine, and how the men who were saved had *retablos* painted to put in the church.

Then I pointed to the picture with my grandfather in it. I said that my grandfather was very brave. If something happened, he would pull the cord that was connected to a bell on the outside, to let people know there was trouble.

And I said that that time the men had dug into an underground stream and a flood had started. My grandfather made them climb on some rocks in the tunnel, while he and another man dug a path for the water to run off. The picture shows the men crouching together and praying, while my grandfather is digging. And in the corner is Santiago (the saint) himself.

The foreigners liked that story. They shook their heads and said, "It was a miracle, wasn't it?"

Then Andreas got an idea. So far he hadn't said anything, but now he asked, "Would you like to

see the mine?"

The man said, "Oh, is the mine still here?"

Andreas said, "Yes. We will show you."

We went out of the church and along the path over the hill. Once it had been a road for wagons, but now, since it was seldom used, it had shrunk to a path. When we got to the door in the wall, we banged on it and waited. We heard the dog barking. We banged and banged, and for a long time nobody came. The lady began to get nervous and said, "Maybe we should go back."

But I banged some more, with a stone, and at last I heard José saying, "Who's there? What do you want?"

I shouted, "Some nice people who want to see the mine."

We heard him slide the bolt back, and the door creaked open and we went in.

José scowled at us. He never was very friendly, but this time he looked quite cross.

He said, "Where are you from, *Señor* and *Señora*?"

They said they were tourists, and that we had told them about the mine, and they would like to see it.

José said, "Well, all right. You see it is closed. There is no more silver. But it is quite dangerous, so I am here to take care of things."

Then he showed us the shaft where the silver was pulled up. It was a hole in the ground with a little wall built around it. José picked up a stone and dropped it down. It took a long time before we heard it hit the bottom.

"You see?" he said. "It's very deep. That's why the door is locked, so people won't come in and fall down."

"Where did the miners go in?" the lady asked.

José pointed to a door that was fastened with a big bolt.

"Can we look in there?" the man asked.

"No, *Señor*," said Jose. "Nobody goes there, not even I. There are tunnels and steps leading into the middle of the earth itself. It is very dangerous."

He showed us a rusty wire with a bell attached. He pulled the wire and the bell jangled.

"The wire goes all the way into the mine," he said. "If there was trouble, the men pulled it and rang the bell."

"And where did they work the silver ore?" the man asked. "I don't see any machinery here."

"No, *Señor,* this was a very small mine," said José. "They took the rocks and ore away to a bigger place where they had very large mills. If you go through the town, maybe you will see it."

Then he pointed out his farm, his corn patch and cactus trees, and his house. The dog barked a few times, but José threw a stone at it and it stopped.

The tourists took some pictures of the farm. But José would not let them take his picture. He frowned and shook his head. The visitors gave him some money, and he let us out.

We walked along the path back to the village. It was quiet and sunny, and not many people were out, just a couple of women getting water and some little kids playing. The visitors took pictures of them, and of the church, and then of me and Andreas standing beside their car. Andreas liked the car very much. He tried not to put his fingers on it, but he did not succeed.

Then the lady said, "I'm very thirsty. Can we buy something to drink?"

We showed her *Señora* Lopez' store, and they bought four bottles of Coca-Cola, and gave one each to me and Andreas. Oh, that was good! But I didn't drink it all. I saved most of it to give to Maria

because she was sick.

The tourists got into the car. The man called us over and said, "This is for you. *Gracias*." And he gave us each five pesos! Then they drove away.

I said to Andreas, "If only tourists would come every day, we would be rich."

But Andreas shook his head and said, "No. But if we could get inside the door to the mine, we might. I bet you there is silver in there."

I said, "Andreas, you are crazy for sure. First of all, you can't just find silver. You have to dig out a lot of rocks, and then grind them up and melt them and the silver runs out. The teacher said so. And besides, José said that even he never goes inside the mine."

Andreas laughed at me. "You believed him? I didn't. Because if he never went inside, the bolt would be rusty. But it wasn't. It was shiny."

I said, "Well, I don't know how you are going to find out, because I bet you José will never let us in there. And anyhow, I'm hungry. I'm going home."

3

I went home almost expecting to find Maria better on account of the *milagro* and the prayers. But she wasn't. So I felt angry again. I thought to myself, "Now look! We prayed and I promised Santiago a *retablo,* and he hasn't done anything."

But then I thought, "Maybe it was he who made the tourists come so that I could earn five pesos! Who knows?"

I gave Maria the Coca-Cola, and she gave some to Rosita. Then I gave Mama the five pesos, and she was pleased. She said, "I will go to *Señora* Lopez and buy something."

She hurried away, and when she came back, she

had chili and beans and also a melon that the Señora had let her have cheap. So we had a good dinner.

But the next day she said, "Santiago, today you must stay home and help. I have to go out to wash."

I was sorry not to go to school again, but it could not be helped. I went for water and I made the fire, and Maria told me how to make soup. Rosita played with the Coca-Cola bottle. She wrapped a rag around it and said it was a doll.

After a while *Tia* Clara came. She said she wanted to see how Maria was feeling, and she brought some tortillas and made some cinnamon tea.

Later Andreas came in. He had been to school, and he said the teacher was asking for me.

I said, "Did you ask him if there could be silver in the mine?"

He said, "No, I didn't want to." Then he looked at *Tia* Clara and asked, "*Señora,* do *you* know if there is any treasure around here?"

Tia Clara laughed and said, "Oh, there are

many stories." And she began to tell us stories.

She sat on a little stool, and Maria lay on her mat, and Rosita played with her bottle and Andreas and I sat on the floor and listened.

Some stories were about things that happened during the Revolution. You see, we had a revolution here in Mexico, when the poor people got tired of being so poor, and decided to change things. And some rich people in our village got scared that all their money would be taken away. So they buried it in the pigpen. Then they ran away. I guess they had so much they couldn't carry it all with them. They thought it was safe, because who would dig in a pigpen? But when they came back, they could not find it. There was no pigpen anymore, and no money. Well, when the village heard of it, everyone started to dig. They dug up the whole street, but the money never appeared.

Then *Tía* Clara told us about some workmen who were knocking down a house and in the wall they found two pots of silver coins. They started to fight over who owned them, and while they were

fighting, someone else ran away with the money.

Andreas asked, "Are those stories true?"

Tía Clara said, "Who knows? They are good stories to laugh at."

Andreas said, "I would not laugh if I found all that money. I would just take it and run."

"Then what would you do?" she asked.

"I would give some to my friends," said Andreas, "and the rest to my parents."

"You are a good boy," said *Tía* Clara, "and I hope you will find some treasure. But I will tell you something. Treasure is not always what you expect. You may not recognize it when you see it. How do you know what treasure is?"

We stared at her, not knowing what she meant. But before we could ask, she began to tell us another story. It was about a man who was so poor that he had nothing to eat, and his children were crying with hunger. His wife told him to go out and find something. So he went out and wandered around in the night, till he came to a mountain. He started to climb up the mountain, thinking, "It is no use. I might as well climb up and sit on the top of this mountain till I die."

But halfway up he came to an opening in the mountain. The doors were wide open, and it was brightly lighted inside. He went in and saw many people. There were piles of delicious foods, just like a market. A man came over and said to him, "Take some, take some."

He said, "But I have no money."

The man said, "It doesn't matter, take whatever you like. But I must warn you, at twelve o'clock the doors will close, and you will have to stay here all night. So hurry up."

So the poor man took a few handfuls of beans and mangoes and some chili peppers and corn, and hurried out.

He ran home to show his wife what he had, but when he took the things out of his pockets they had turned to silver! So now they were rich and could buy anything they wanted.

Well, the next day his neighbor came to see him. The neighbor was also poor, and when he saw all the good things on the table he asked, "How did you get so rich?"

The man said, "I went to the mountain and got lots of silver. Come with me tonight and I will show you." So that night he took him to the opening in the mountain, and explained that he had to leave before twelve o'clock. But the neighbor didn't listen. He just ran in looking for silver, but he couldn't find any. He asked people, "Where is the silver?" And they said, "We haven't any." Because you see, there wasn't any silver there.

By and by the doors were closed, and he didn't even notice. So he had to stay there all night. And when morning came, and the doors were opened, and he went out, all he had was a handful of vegetables. He went home and his wife scolded him, asking, "Where have you been all this time?"

"What's the matter?" he said. "Can't I even stay out one night?"

"One night!" she said. "You've been gone a whole year!"

I thought that was a very sad story. Perhaps the man was greedy, but still it was mean to punish him so much.

Then Maria said, "I wish my Papa would come home, even if he only brings us a few vegetables."

That made me feel so sad, I didn't want to stay in the house any more. I said to Andreas, "Come on, let's go." And we went outside. I was tired of all this talk about silver. I wanted to do something, but I couldn't think what to do.

Then I noticed the plum tree. It was covered

with ripe plums. It gave me an idea.

I said, "Andreas, you know what? Every year my father picks the plums, and this year he had no time. He went away and didn't do it. Let's pick the plums and sell them."

Andreas said, "But everybody in the village has plums."

I said, "Well, what about the market? There is a market in town tomorrow."

Our own village is too small for a market, except on fiesta days. So when we want to go to market, we have to walk to town.

Andreas said, "All right, I'll go with you."

We started picking plums, and we got four bags full. Two we gave to our mothers for drying. Then we told our mothers we wanted to go to town, and they said we could, so we started early the next day. Each of us had a bag of plums, and we started out walking fast, to get there early and get a good place. But Ay! those bags were heavy, and the sun began to get warm.

Andreas said, "If only we had a burro!"

I said, "Why don't you wish for a blue automobile while you are at it? Maybe some saint would give you one."

But the saints were busy somewhere else. because no automobile came along. So we walked all the way to town.

In the market, we put our bags of plums on the sidewalk and pulled the tops open so people could see them. Then we sat down and waited for customers. But for a long time nobody bought, so we watched the people.

There were crowds of people in the market. I like to go there, there is always something to see. On the sidewalk were women selling vegetables, little piles of beans and rice, oranges arranged in pyramids, and bunches of flowers. One woman had a few cactus fruits spread in front of her. And in the regular market, under the canopies, were people selling potatoes and tomatoes and peppers and shoes and rebozos and hats.

I thought, "If we earn a lot of money, maybe

I felt bad because in a way it was my fault. But Andreas saw a woman cooking beans in a little stove on the sidewalk, so he went and bought a tortilla and some beans with his five centavos, and each of us ate half. Ay, they were good! Then we were thirsty.

A man walked by selling ice cream and shouting, *"Helado, helado, helado!"* It looked awfully good, but we had no more money, so we ate some plums.

A couple of tourist ladies walked by, looking around at everything.

Suddenly Andreas gave me a poke and said, "Look there! Who is that?"

An old man in a black serape, with a sombrero pulled over his face, was walking through the market. He seemed to be selling something. He walked up to the tourists and showed them something he had in his hand.

I said, "It looks like José."

"It *is* José," said Andreas. "I wonder what he has there."

The tourist lady looked surprised and asked José something. Then she took out money and paid him, and put the thing, whatever it was, in her bag.

Then she wanted to take a picture of him. But he shook his head and walked away. Well, that was not surprising, lots of people don't like to have their pictures taken. But I was dying to know what he had sold the lady.

Andreas said, "I bet you it's silver. He has found some in the mine and now he is selling it."

It seemed as if Andreas had silver on the brain.

"I'm going to follow him and see," he said. So he ran off while I stayed with the plums.

I thought, "Well, Santiago, how about a little luck now?" (I was talking to my saint, not myself.)

And just then I did have luck. Not much, but a little. The same tourist lady came over and wanted to take a picture of me sitting on the pavement with my plums. So I let her. I wished I could ask her what she had bought from José, but I wasn't brave enough. But when she got through taking pictures, she opened her bag, and I could not help looking inside. I expected to see something shining like silver in there, but I did not. There were just a lot of things, a purse and a handkerchief, and something the color of mud. I didn't know what it was, but I thought it was a funny thing for a lady to buy. She opened the purse and gave me a peso and went away.

Andreas came back saying, "I didn't find out a thing. He walked around a corner and when I got there he was gone."

He was very disappointed. So I gave him the peso and told him to buy us some ice cream. That made us both feel better.

We sold most of our plums, and then it was time to go home. Most of the market people were packing up their stuff, calling their children, and loading their baskets on their backs.

The woman with the cactus fruits was still sitting there. Nobody would buy them now, because they looked dirty and stale, but she still looked up at everybody who went past. So I gave her the rest of the plums, and Andreas and I started for home. I thought we had not done too badly. We had some money and the tomatoes I had picked up, and we had eaten, and seen many things. But Andreas was not satisfied. All the way home I could see that he was thinking about what to do next.

4

The next day Andreas came to my house early.

"Are you going to school?" he asked.

I said, "No, I don't want to." I really did want to, and Maria was a little better so I could have gone. But somehow when you stop going it's hard to get started again.

He said, "Well, I'm not going either. I'm going to watch José and see what he does."

I said, "Andreas, you're crazy. You better go to school. You'll just make him mad, and then you'll be in trouble."

But he ran off. Later when I went to the fountain for water, I could see him hiding around the corner of the church wall, where he could see the path that led to the mine. He was not doing anything, just sitting there on the ground.

I went home, and soon he came running after me. "Come on, quick, he's gone!"

"Who's gone?" I asked.

"José. He came from the mine on his burro and he's gone out of the village. Come on. Help me get in."

"Get in where?" I asked.

"Over the wall. I want to see if I can get the mine door open."

I didn't want to. Because what if José suddenly decided to come back and found us there? I didn't know what he would do to us. But I couldn't let Andreas go alone, so I went with him. We hurried along the path to the mine, and there was the wall in front of us with the big door in it. I tried the door. It was locked. I looked up at the wall. It was terribly high. I didn't see how we could ever climb it.

Andreas said, "Bend down and let me climb

on your back." So I did, and he stood on my back and then on my shoulders, and even then he could not reach the top of the wall. Inside, we could hear the dog barking. Andreas jumped down.

"It's no use," I said. "You better forget it."

We went back to the village. I wanted to cheer him up so I said, "Look, maybe we can go and work for *Señor* Salvador again." (He was the farmer who hired us to cut corn for him.)

Andreas said, "All right."

I said, "You go and ask him. I have to go home now."

Señor Salvador said we could take his cow up on the hill and watch her. So the next morning we went for the cow.

"You be sure to watch her," he said. "Don't let her wander off. She likes to go for a walk. That's why I keep her tied up. And don't let a *nahual* come near her." (A *nahual* is a bad spirit that likes to steal things.)

I knew he was joking because he smiled and

gave us each a couple of tortillas that his wife had just made. He was a nice man.

We led the cow up on the hill and sat down to watch her eat grass and corn stalks.

I liked it up there. I felt close to the sky, as if I could almost touch the white clouds that the wind was pushing along. But Andreas was looking down, and suddenly he said, "Santiago, look! There is José on his burro coming along the path. He's going somewhere again! Oh, if only I could get in there!"

I said, "Well, we are supposed to watch the cow, not to go exploring." Then I looked around. Where *was* the cow? She had disappeared.

"The cow is gone!" I shouted. "Andreas, weren't you watching her?"

He said, "No, I thought you were."

We started running all around looking for the cow.

I said, "She must have gone down the other side of the hill." So we ran that way. The bushes were thick there, and halfway down there was a fence to keep people and animals away, which was why we never went there for firewood. We came to the fence, and I saw that it was broken. The cow must have gone through, looking for better pasturage. We could see where the branches and the grasses were crushed. We followed the trail downward, and there was the cow, eating from a flowering bush.

"You're a bad cow," I said to her, taking hold of her halter and starting to lead her back up the hill.

But Andreas said, "Wait!"

"What's the matter?" I asked.

"I found something," he said. "Tie the cow to a tree and come down here."

I tied her so that she could go on eating but couldn't get away, and followed Andreas down the path. I heard him, but I couldn't see him.

"Where are you?" I called.

"Down here, below the rocks," he said.

Then I saw that there was a ledge of rock, sticking out of the hillside like a roof. Andreas was underneath it. I went down to him.

"Look what I found," he said. There was an old shovel with a broken handle, and a hole where somebody had been digging. Andreas was on his hands and knees, feeling in the dirt with his fingers. "I found something," he said. And he held up a broken piece of a clay cup. It was black, with a streak of red paint. He looked at it with disgust. "I thought I would find something good," he said.

I started to dig too. Soon I found another

piece like the first one. But then Andreas took the shovel, in order to dig faster.

"I've got something!" he said, and then he gave a yell. It was a bone! There was a skeleton there!

"Dios mío!" he shouted. "Let's get out of here! Somebody's been murdered!" And he crossed himself.

But I said, "No, I don't think so. These are old bones. I think somebody was buried here very long ago."

Then I picked out from the dirt a little thing. It looked like a doll made of clay.

Andreas said, "That would be good for your sister Rosita to play with. I thought we would find treasure, but it's just this junk."

I dug some more. I found a bowl with three legs, and some broken pieces, and then a jar. It was shaped like a bird, the lower part round, and a small round part stuck on top for a head. The head was painted with two big eyes and a beak.

"It looks like an owl," I said.

But Andreas was not interested in broken dishes or even in owls.

He had discovered something else.

"See," he said, "there is a path leading down to the mine. This is the way to get there, not over the wall. Now is our chance to see what's there. I'm going down."

"No, don't," I said. But he was scrambling down the hill. I heard the dog barking, and I called, "Come back!" But he wouldn't, so I had to go with him. I put the little doll in my pocket, and I put the owl carefully against a tree trunk so it wouldn't break, and I went quickly after Andreas. The goat looked at us, and the dog barked. José had thrown a stone to shut him up, but I gave him a tortilla and that satisfied him.

Andreas walked straight to the mine door and slid back the bolt. It moved easily, as if it had been oiled. We looked in. It was dark and smelled of musty earth, and I could dimly see the tunnel stretching away into the blackness. For a minute I thought of my grandfather, going in there every day, and it made me shiver.

Andreas took a step forward, as if he were going in, but I pulled him back and said, "No, don't go in."

"But I want to see if there's treasure," he said.

"Look there," I told him. Just inside the door was a basket, and in it were some more of the little clay dolls, and a couple of three-legged bowls.

He said, "You mean this is it?"

I said, "Yes. Now I know what I saw in the market, in that lady's bag. It was one of those little dolls that José sold her. He's the one who has been digging, and selling what he finds. Come on. Let's go, before he comes back."

I pushed the door shut and we ran back to the hill and climbed as fast as we could. I felt scared, as though something were chasing me. We untied the cow and led her back over the hill to the pasture, and tied her so she would not break through the fence again. Then we sat down to catch our breath.

Andreas laughed. "It's good you didn't let me go down in the mine," he said. "It looked too much like that hole in the mountain *Tía* Clara told about. I might have had to stay there a year."

I said, "Yes, and what would I tell your mother?"

"What a strange thing," said Andreas. "All the time I thought the old man had found silver or money."

"Silver or money would be different," I said. "But I don't think it's right to dig where somebody is buried. I don't know."

"What shall we do?" he asked.

I said, "We must talk to the teacher. He will know."

We untied the cow and led her home. The farmer said, "I can't give you any money, but here are some plums."

Andreas said, "*Gracias, Señor,* but we have plums. Perhaps you have something else for us?"

Señor Salvador smiled and said, "Like some more tortillas?" And he went into the house and asked his wife for tortillas for us. He also gave us some milk to drink.

Then we went to the teacher's house.

It was nearly suppertime, but I thought, "We must go now, or José will come back and maybe he will see that somebody has been there. If we tell the teacher now, he will protect us."

The teacher was starting to eat his supper. He said, "Come in, boys. You haven't been to school lately. What have you been doing?"

I said, "We were working because our fathers have gone away. And today, when we were guarding *Señor* Salvador's cow, we found something. We thought you would know what it is." And I took out the little doll.

5

The teacher jumped up as if a bee had stung him.

"Dios mío!" he shouted. "Where did you find this?"

"Up over the hill," I told him. "We were following the cow, and there are some rocks there, and underneath we saw that somebody had been digging, so we dug too, and we found this and some broken dishes and some bones."

"But this is tremendous!" he said. "It must be a burial. This is very old. Who knows? You may have made a discovery."

Andreas said, "What is it? Isn't it just a doll?"

The teacher answered, "No, Andreas, it's an

idol, a little image of a god, perhaps. The people used to put these into the graves to help the dead on their way to the next world. And they left bowls with food and jars with flowers or water."

"What were the jars like?" I asked.

"Sometimes they had faces," he said. "Sometimes they were shaped like animals or birds. But why are we sitting here? You must take me there at once. Nobody must dig any more. We must get an archaeologist from the city. Nothing must be moved."

I said, "But, *Señor,* some things have already been moved. José has taken some. We looked in the mine itself and found more of them in a basket."

"He's sold some," said Andreas.

"What!" shouted the teacher. "How do you know?"

"We saw him in the market," I said.

"It's against the law," said the teacher. "These are our national treasures."

Andreas said, "*Señor,* you told us there were

no treasures around here. We were looking for treasure, but we didn't know that little clay dolls and broken dishes were so valuable."

The teacher sat down again. He wiped his face with his handkerchief and calmed down a little.

Then he said, "When I said that, I meant there were no great pyramids or magnificent carvings. But you see, here and there we find the places where plain simple people lived, people like you and me. They lived and died and were buried, and from the burials we learn about them. We learn how they lived, what they ate, what they believed. They were our ancestors. But to study them, we must find them where they are lying. That's why it is wrong to dig these things out and sell them. Now come, we must go."

But I said, "*Señor,* we have not been home yet. We have not had supper. And besides, it will soon be dark."

"You are right, boy," said the teacher. "Come back tomorrow. Then we will go."

We went home. I felt very tired. My mother

and Maria asked me where I had been and why I was so tired, but I did not tell them. I only said I had been working for *Señor* Salvador. Soon after supper I lay down on my mat and went to sleep.

It was lucky that the next day was Saturday, so there was no school. We went to the teacher's house early. We wanted to take him over the hill the way we went, but he said, "No, it is better to go to José directly." So we went along the path and banged on the door. We had to bang a long time, but at last José came. Andreas and I were scared, but the teacher was not afraid at all.

He said, "*Señor,* I am sorry to disturb you, but it has come to my notice that there may be an ancient burial somewhere here. Can you tell me about it?"

José said, "This is the property of the mine owners. Nobody is allowed here. Nobody could have found anything here."

"Except you, *Señor,*" said the teacher. "I am glad to hear it. You know it is against the law

to dig or sell ancient things. Of course you would not break the law."

"Me?" shouted José. "Are you accusing me?"

"No. I am asking you to help me," said the teacher.

So we went in, and José scowled at us, but he couldn't prevent us from showing the teacher where to look. First he looked inside the mine entrance. José didn't want him to open the door but he did anyhow, and there was the basket.

The teacher picked it up and said, "*Señor,* I see you understand the value of these things and have taken good care of them. I will take them with me to be sure nothing happens to them."

And he carefully put the little dolls and the bowls in a box that he had with him. José looked angry, but he didn't say a word. Then we went up the path and pointed out the place under the rock ledge. The teacher had a little shovel, and he began to dig, very carefully. He got so excited that I was afraid he would fall down the hill.

He found the skeleton, but did not touch it. Instead he covered it up again; and then he picked out a bowl that had some little bits of bone in the bottom.

"See," he said, "this was meat that was put there for this person to eat on his journey. The bowl is a type that was made more than two thousand years ago. *Muchachos,* it is a great discovery."

He carefully covered everything up, and we went back down the path. José asked, "Well, *Señor,* did you find anything?"

"Yes," said the teacher, "some ancient bones and pottery of much value. And now I must go to town to telephone. We will get an expert from the city to come and work here, and we will get the police to come and guard the place, so that nothing happens to it. And meanwhile you, *Señor,* can see that nobody comes near, so that nothing is disturbed. And now good morning."

José said, "But what about those things you took? Are you going to keep them?"

The teacher said, "I will show them to the authorities. Perhaps you will get a reward when I tell them you found them."

We went out and heard the bolt slide shut.

The teacher got his car, and we went with him to town. It was a good ride. He drove very fast and almost hit a few things, but with God's help we got there safely.

The teacher telephoned and then started back.

I said, "But you said you were going to the police, *Señor*."

He laughed. "That was just to frighten José. I do not think we will need the police."

And sure enough, when we returned and went back to the mine, the door was not locked. We went in and found nobody but the goat. José, the burro and the dog were gone.

José never came back. But some archaeologists came. They came from the museum in the city, and they examined everything, and then they decided to dig on the hillside. But first some men came to fix the road so that cars could come in. And best of all, my father and Andreas' father came home. They got jobs on the road, and later at the dig.

The archaeologists said it was a good dig, because they found things that showed how the people lived—tools and pottery and even some bits of cloth and basketwork.

They worked most of the winter, until it was time for planting again. Andreas and I worked there too, when we were not in school. We carried water to the men, and helped them carry away dirt, and I learned the right way to dig, very carefully so as not to spoil anything, but to uncover everything just as it lay in the earth. I like this work. I hope the men will come back. Maybe when I grow up I'll be an archaeologist.

With the first money I earned, I bought Rosita a real doll, and after that I bought my mother a new rebozo. And now I am saving up for a *retablo* for Santiago, because I promised him one.

But to tell the truth, I am not perfectly sure it was he who did it all. Sometimes I think it was someone else. You see, I did something that I should not have done. The little owl that I found that first day, and hid behind a tree— well, I did not put him back. I know I should have, and maybe sometime I will. But I loved him so much that I wanted to keep him awhile. I found a secret place for him, that nobody knows

about except me. And I put him there, and sometimes I bring him things. Flowers and a piece of a tortilla and things like that. I guess it's wrong to keep him, but perhaps not as wrong as to sell him, as José would have done.

I asked *Tía* Clara once if owls meant anything special, and she said, "Yes, the owl is the bird of death."

Maybe that is why he was put with the dead person in the grave. So I am a little bit scared of him. But then again, maybe he is the one who brought us luck, and if I treat him well he will bring more. Who knows?